Whispers on th Road to Peace

By Sally Sparrow

Contents

Treasure 4
Sunflower 6
Faint Importance 7
Swimming Club 9
Daisy 10
Integrated Development and Learning Environment 11
Sunshine 12
Of Pigs and Dogs 14
Narcissus 16
Dog 19
See me 20
The Devil's Gluten Free Biscuits 22
Is it wrong 24
Swelling 24
Smarties 24
Crown of Thorns 25
Breathe 27
Precipice 30
Golden 32
Silence 33
Cattle 35
Onwards 36
Solitude 36

Dichotomy	37
Absence	39
Alone	40
Superior	41
Untamed	42
Flimsy	43
:)	45
My Crown	46
It's fine	47
My Garden	50
Another Sunflower	52
Sunflower II	53
All roads	54
Ashes	56
Uncontrollable	58
Blossom	61
Sunglasses and Rum	62
Colonising Planets with my Sunflower	63
Brightly	65
Cloudless Skies	66
The Sun with Sunglasses	67

Treasure

The end of the day,
I hate it a little less.
It gets easier,
I miss you a little less.

And it hurts to think,
one day I might not even
think about you once.

my worst fear was to lose you,
you were once my light.

but now, it is me
forgetting to think of you.

living my nightmare
I'll recall our golden days,
I'll pretend you're here.

I won't promise you I will,
I promise to try
remember you til I die.

because I loved you

and you were my saviour

I cannot risk it

golden treasure chest of my

memories with you,

the only thing I value.

even if I do,

risk the treasure chest of us,

even if I lose,

I will never not love you.

I swear on my life,

even when my heart gives in,

it will beat for you.

Sunflower

We laugh, we fight
You're the sunflower
In my green plains.

You are the most important piece
In this landscape.

Countless superior experiences,
only had with you.

So bright, so lovely,
I am always overjoyed to see you.

Your euphoric yellow
stains all of my memories.

Faint Importance

Blurred, are my memories of you

The importance now but just

A murky feeling

I remember your name,

I remember all the stuff we did,

but your importance and

relevance and place

and home in my heart…

How can I explain it?

It's duller, plainer

The memories are bland,

Matter-of-fact

No longer as cherished or

As golden

My treasure chest has

Turned from gold to

Dirt and I don't know what to do

To make myself care

It is what it is, nothing lasts

So why is there a part of me that hurts so much?
A part of me that just wants to hug you again,
to see you and smile and laugh and dance?

The waters of my mind are murky-
Nothing is clear anymore and I don't know what to do.

Maybe I have one clarity-
I miss you

Swimming Club

life is a lake

and we're all drifting in it

trying not to drown

I wonder if anyone really ever escapes it

when we die, we sink

and reside forevermore at the bottom

you can excel in it, sure

but the bottom will consume us all

and the water will be the same after you've sunk

so where's the point in your drifting,

in your trying,

in your very presence?

Daisy

a daisy is picked

worn in a little girls hair

then it's discarded

discarded and left

alone to wither away

erode into dirt

Integrated Development and Learning Environment

we live to die

we die to live

circles and circles

pain and happiness

joy and suffering

everything passes

nothing remains

thus nothing matters

in the midst of all the meaningless,

in the midst of the nothingness,

We can find even more useless things,

and somehow find a value in them.

Even though this gold will also decay,

into a lump of shit

Sunshine

The sun still shines,

Even if I'm struggling,

Even if I'm alone,

Even if it feels like nothing matters,

The sun is still shining.

How can I worry about anything when

The sun shines?

The clouds glow?

The grass is always greener;

So why worry?

The sun will outlive me;

It will be a constant in my life-

It will never waver or vanish

It will still be shining long after I'm gone

My great grandkids will look at the same sun

My ancestors looked at the same sun too;

The same sun shone on their crops

Kept them warm and well fed

In the grand scheme my worries are nothing
Because the sun is still shining

Of Pigs and Dogs

In the farmhouse the pigs are fed and bred,

They exist for our benefit only.

They are alive only because we allow them to be

They exist to die

They are born to be slaughtered

And eaten

They live their lives rolling in mud

Attempting to be happy

While knowing they exist to die

They were only allowed to live

so they could be fattened up

To feed the families of their captors

The dogs must work or be put down

They exist only to keep the sheeps together

The dogs must work always

They get a little treat when they do their job

The pigs and the dogs are the same

Born to die

Does anything matter if living has an unavoidable end?

Narcissus

I want attention;

especially from you

I just want your affection;

I want to feel like you love me

I want to hear you say sweet things;

I don't want to feel like you're pretending out of pity

I'm tired of feeling like everyone is faking everything

I'm so tired

I just want you to stop hating me

I just want to feel loved

I feel like if I kill myself

You'll love me more

I'll have all the attention and affection if I'm dead

If I'm dead I won't have to worry

About people hating me

Or the memory of me

I just want to kill myself;

specifically for you

Specifically to make you show affection for me

If I'm dead I won't need to think

I'll be dead, the reality of
You hating me still
Will be unknown to me
If I were dead I could continue living in my
delusions
That you didn't hate me
That you didn't think of me as a waste of oxygen

Why can't you love me?
What did I ever do to you?
I've known you and been by your side for 18 years,
Why are you hurting me so much?
Why can't we live in peace? Why can't you just love me?

I just want your affection
I just want to be loved by you
Nobody else matters; if the world hates me I want
at least you to love me.
But you don't for the sake of humility;
For the sake of humility you hate me

Why can't you be like Narcissus?
Why can't you look at me and love me dearly?

Why can't you kill yourself for me?

But you can't because you don't love me enough

And even if you killed yourself I would still hate you

You're always pretending it's all okay

when really you just want

their attention and affection

Did your parents not coddle you enough as a child?

Why do you seek the

approval and attention of others

Rather than that from myself?

So stop worrying

About anyone except me

Dog

Jump doggy, jump!

Fetch doggy, fetch!

Roll over!

Good boy!

Here's a treat for your hard work today!

See you tomorrow, doggy!

See me

See me see me see me

Whining in my head

I ignore the voices

I pray them dead

See me see me see me

They cry and cry and cry

Nobody sees me nobody loves me

They whine and whine

I plead for their silence

I pray for their demise

But my prayers fall on deaf ears,

My prayers go to Gods with no sentience, I suppose

See me see me see me

They nag and nag and nag

Pleading for your attention,

pleading for your love

I beg for their silence

I ask for them to depart

But again I speak

To nothing but brick and mortar

They cry and whine about the unwavering truth of existence;

That is that it is ultimately meaningless

I fight with them

I will continue to fight with them

Until God sees fit to remove me

and them from this earth

The Devil's Gluten Free Biscuits

There is nothing

There is nothing

Then

Yellow light gently falls in

You are truly

A gift from God

I'll never be able to repay either of you,

For the taking these horrible feelings away

I could sing a thousand songs

About how good you are

And I could play a million more

About how good God is

for letting me meet you

At my darkest moments you were there,

Pulling me back from the edge

I will never be able to repay you

I could devote my whole life to serving you

I could give you every penny I have ever earned

I could write a thousand poems

And I could make a million sculptures

Nothing will ever come close to repaying

The gift of your time and your presence

Yellow bleeds through,

The darkness is no longer closing in,

And I sigh in relief

If God won't let me die I want to spend everyday with you

Is it wrong

I will be okay

If everyone will hate me

As long as you don't

Swelling

A swelling feeling

That I can never escape

Kills me so gently

Smarties

In a world of lots,

your existence is worthless

this fact should bring peace

Crown of Thorns

This little garden of mine,

It's overgrown

Weeds and flowers alike,

They all blossom

I cannot help but love them,

I cannot help but pour my very soul into them

I want them to bloom,

I'll love them to death

My garden is dying because

I don't have enough soul

Thorns stab me,

The spiders poison me,

Never ending their assaults

Is this what Newton had in mind,

When he theorised his third law?

Is the immense and painful love I have for you,

Met with an equally intense hatred for me?

I can do nothing but pour more of myself,
Into your thorns

I can do nothing,
but love you

I want you all to flourish,
Even if your thorns
tear the flesh off my bones

More, more, more
Take all of me
Let me die in this little garden

Weeds and flowers alike,
I will love and serve you
by even my death
If that is what will appease you

Breathe

In but just one breath

I am alone

The ocean of my mind

Is drowning me

I can think of nothing

Except an action I cannot take

In, hold, out

Just like the internet told me to

The breathing does not soothe

The pain I am in

I am alone in this world

In, hold, out

The pain is incessant

If I ignore it

It will simply drown me later

In hold out

It hurts and I hurt

and I want to hurt more

In hold out

Nothing matters

In hold out

Nobody cares

In hold out

I am a burden on society

In hold out

In hold out

In hold out

I want to be loved

And I wish I deserved love

In hold out

A useless piece of shit

In hold out

You can't even keep yourself happy

In hold out

You are a fat piece of shit

In hold out

You are disgusting

In hold out

In hold out

Is it over?

Precipice

Misty, dark and clouded

I smell rain, and

For once I am at peace

I close my eyes,

Knowing there is nothing

But a fall in front of me

Breathing deeply,

Completely at ease

With my future

A darkness so deep,

A silence so inviting,

An end that smells so refreshing

There is a waterfall nearby,

I can hear the water

As it splashes down below

And though I cannot see it,

It is so inviting

It is so tempting

Dewy air, deep silence,
And I am ready.

Then I hear a birdsong so loud and piercing and beautiful;
It shakes me from my daze.

And I realise the silence is gloomy,
the smell of the rain is rancid,
the water is crashing loudly,
the end of the abyss is far from peaceful.

Astounded by these awakenings,
I hurriedly turn from what I was about to do.

Nodding a short thanks
to the white dove,
that saved my life,
yet again.

Golden

they say that clouds have a silver lining,

but when the sun sets--

their lining dies,

the cloud itself turns into gold--

most of it, anyways.

Then, you blink

and the lining is again silver

but in that moment,

when the sun is setting,

the cloud is gold

Silence

The silence that once ravaged

And destroyed my peace

Now provides comfort to me

It was once dark and

violating to be in

leeching on my skin

Equipped with needles and knives,

With one desire

of mutilating my soul

It comforts me now,

Silence so stabilising

I know it well now

He is still my enemy

But I know his plans

His evils ground me

A silence that stabs,

Is better than

A noise that numbs

Cattle

The cow is tired,

Of being mindlessly slaughtered.

It wants to be behind the curtain;

It's had enough of being mindless property.

What does the cow need to do

to escape the fields and the herd?

Where does the cow run

to experience unrestricted freedom?

The mindless cow is moving in the dark,

Unguided, driven by instinct alone.

Mindless cow,

How far do you believe you can go?

Onwards

with a great courage,

Running head first into pain,

I won't hide from this

Solitude

There's no unity,

Even in community,

You're wholly alone.

Dichotomy

Let us analyse the human condition
Or at least a human's condition

There can be a discrepancy
Between the health of the mind
And the health of the body

A mind desiring to die lives in a body,
more than capable of living
And lives a life more than worthy of living

There was no cause or reason for this urge to die;
No life threatening illness,
No trauma or bruises or scars,
A perfectly healthy body and life

And yet this mind has one unchanging plan
the soul is withering and yet the body
The body flourishes.

The body works so hard to keep this mind alive,
This mind that doesn't want to exist.

Is God cruel to let the body live,
despite the mind's pleas for death?

'Yet not I but through Christ in me'
The other bodies sing,
their minds eager to live another day

And the body sings,
This mind asking for strength not to make this day
The body's last.

This mind prays again, asking for release
from this meaningless existence
And the body sings along

'Yet not I but through Christ in me'
The thoughts hesitate, almost completely stop
Until tomorrow this mind is at peace.

Absence

Once again I am alone,

And I have the power to end the voice

That never quiets

It rages and whines and pleads,

With me

To end it

I want to end it,

But I won't

If the voice wants to die,

Then I will force it to live

Maybe if it wasn't

such a self-absorbed cow

I would do it the favour.

Alone

I blink and my sun is gone;
There's nothing for me to orbit,
No stabilising source of gravity.

I'm left to drift along the dark universe,
Alone and lightless.

Time moves on but how many days pass,
I will never know.

My sun is gone, and
there's no joy in living anymore.

There may have been
thousands of stars in the galaxy,
But you were my sun,
Not even Jupiter could trump you.

Slowly everything I am dies;
There is no life without you.

My sun, why did you leave?

Superior

You and I are superior together,
The best of friends,
The strongest companions

I never believed in soulmates;
upon further review I was wrong

Our relationship is exclusively platonic and yet
So much more than platonic

I love you more than a platonic love
And greater than a familial love
And yet greater still than a romantic love

I wouldn't die for you,
I would live for you.

How did I get so lucky,
To find someone I care about
as much as I care about you

Untamed

A rabid animal has more control,

The stormy seas experience a greater peace,

Than this heart of mine.

You could die for me,

You could kill for me,

You could love me,

You could despise me,

I will still chase after you,

I will still idolise you.

My heart will long for you endlessly,

Unconditionally.

Flimsy

Our kinship is strong and mighty,
Absolutely no wave could upturn our ship.

There's not a shark in the sea,
A wave in the ocean,
A stowaway onboard,
That could part thee from me.

There's not a word you could utter,
Not an action you could take,
To turn my affectionate eye,
Away from your face.

This ship of ours is strong,
Built and maintained by a power higher than ourselves,
Therefore we ourselves need nothing.

Take care of yourself,
Allow me to care of you if any need arises,
And I will do so as well.

Our ship will never sink this way;
But even if it did, I firmly believe

We could safely swim back to the shore together,

And rebuild the ship that we lost.

:)

Thoughts invade my head,

Unsolicited they stab me

My brain bleeds,

And I pray to god

For the thoughts to stop

They don't,

They stab more and

My brain bleeds more

I hope I don't drown

in the blood of my mind

My Crown

My brain dwells in a little garden,

Lush and green and alive.

The Gods of this garden have given me a crown-

A crown formed from the branches of a rose bush.

Delicate grey roses

adorn this crown.

The garden is beautiful, the crown is stunning,

Yet my brain bleeds.

The dark shadows of the roses

hide the thorns of the branch.

This crown is placed upon my brain,

The thorns holding it securely in place.

My brain bleeds and bleeds,

And this blood slowly poisons the garden.

It's fine

It hurts me so much and I can't
Breathe when I think of it
And I can't think of anything except it
And it hurts and I'm hurting
And it's fine because it's fine

And it's okay that I'm hurting and it's
Fine

It's fine that I'm not thinking
Because it's fine that I'm hurting

And everything is fine
And it's okay that nothing is fine
And it's fine that nothing is okay

And it's all okay and it's all fine
Because nothing is okay and nothing is fine

And I can't breathe and I can't think
And the only thing I feel is pain but
It's fine and it's okay

And yeah I'm good I'm just crackling

And it's fine because it's not fine
And it's okay because it's not okay
And it's always good because it's never good

And it's just fine and
it's just good and
it's just okay

And I'm hurting and I
Want to hurt so much more

And it's just fine
Because I'm just fine

And it's okay because
It's not okay

And I just want to
And it's just fine

And I just want to be fine and
I'll never be fine

And if I even stop to think
Or process my thoughts

I'm not fine and it's not fine
But it's fine and it's okay
And I'm okay and I'm good

And I don't need to think and
I will be okay and it will be fine

My Garden

My little garden in the valley,

Is small but growing

The flowers are beautiful,

The trees are tall

There is a stream of water,

The source of it is unknown

This stream allows my garden to grow,

I no longer need to pour my soul into it.

Bruised, scarred and yet I am healing

In this little garden in the valley

The water feeds the flowers,

The water provides all they need

They require nothing from me,

They're draining nothing from me

I lie down in this little garden in the valley,

Completely utterly at peace with existence

Another Sunflower

You smile at me,

And everything fades away

How can anything have meaning beside you?

Your smile is beautiful,

Lights up the world itself

How can anyone be sad in your presence?

You speak and my fears fade,

I think of nothing but goodness

when you're near

I want to live inside your head

I never want to go a day without you

I want to be by your side until the end of time

You are a beautiful sunflower and

I want to be your ladybug

Precious, pretty sunflower

Let me live with you forever

Sunflower II

My special precious sunflower

I cannot see how you are growing

I can only pray you'll bloom beautifully

All roads

All roads lead to Rome,

A thousand roads taking us

Forever to Rome.

The life you live,

The journey you undergo,

The people you hurt and are hurt by,

Lead you forever to Rome.

Does this make the roads taken meaningless,

If they all lead to Rome?

Certainly not,

For if not for the roads,

What would take us to Rome?

Perhaps the decisions,

and road you chose is meaningless,

As it will lead you to the same Rome.

However the roads themselves,

These roads hold value;

For they lead us to Rome.

On and upward, my friend!

We haven't reached Rome yet,

Our journey has just begun.

Ashes

There is nothing left
All of it has been reduced to ashes

Not a single soul remains
Not a single building stands

My world is nothing but ashes
And yet from these ashes I will build
From these ashes I will raise life
I will build an unbreakable house

What can destroy my happiness
If there's nothing but the ashes and I?

What can cause my house to crumble
If there's nothing but the ashes and I?

In solitude I was brought into the world
And in solitude I'll depart from it

Therefore solitude is an absolute
Nothing can deprive me of it

In solitude I will build

In solitude I will grow

So when in solitude I die

I will feel no regrets

Uncontrollable

With a rage so uncontrollable,

I try rip the Sun from the sky

I shoot nuclear missiles,

I throw great asteroids

And yet the Sun stands.

The Sun I chose

The Sun that comforted me

It comforts me no longer

It exists out of my reach

I was never tall enough to reach the Sun

The yellow light falls,

The warm rays nothing but a bitter reminder

Of how absolutely undeniably

Useless I am

Yellow light that comforted,

Is now bright and stabbing

Bringing nothing but pain

I rip my eyes out of my head to avoid
Seeing it

And yet the Sun still shines
And yet the warmth I still feel

I rip the skin from my body
And even then I will never forget you

Even if I kill myself,
Will I ever escape the memory of you?

This uncontrollable rage I feel,
At the fact our friendship has failed

This ship greater than us has sunken and
You giggled as I drowned

This rage I don't know where to direct,
At myself for drowning

Or at you for giggling

I am angry.

Why am I never enough?

I choose myself
Over and over exactly as I should have
Exactly as I wish I had

I choose myself
I am selfishly finally
Embracing myself finally

Truly and deeply
I do not care about anyone except me

I will be my own Sun

Blossom

Beautiful flower, you're no longer

An unopened bud

Beautiful flower, you've become

So much more beautiful

With every day that passes

With every flower you grow into

I can think of only one truth about you

And that is that I love you

Sunglasses and Rum

Summertime sunshines light our path;

Tropical shirts and sunglasses decorate our bodies.

And in our minds groovy tunes play on repeat;

Neither of us know what was acceptable in the 80s.

What great adventures we've had,

Mere reflections of the adventures we will have.

Every word we exchange,

Every joke we share,

I am reminded of how thankful I am for you.

My life is no longer meaningless,

God made me live so I could meet you.

My beautiful boy, my shining sunflower,

Let's spend eternity together.

Colonising Planets with my Sunflower

My sunflower,

I want to find the best soils for you,

I want to find the brightest star for you,

I want to give you the best in this existence.

I will find a way to travel to far away galaxies,

I will take you to the best alien planet for sunflowers.

Together we will travel for millenia,

Searching in solitude for a planet to bring life to.

Me and my sunflower will be known all around the universe;

The one-eyed and million-eyed aliens will all know us well.

We will travel and traverse the nothingness until we find the best planet;

Stopping at alien bars and travel lodges,

Trying their cuisine and drink (in spite of their odd smell and flavour)

And when we reach it-

The best planet orbiting the best Star and with the best soil

And the best waters and the best atmosphere

You will grow and thrive and together we will make…

A sunflower planet!

In the best conditions you'll grow and multiply;

Covering the whole planet with your Sunflower clones

What a planet that will be,

How lucky will we be to live on it!

Brightly

Brightly you shine,

The days with and without you are equally bright.

Perhaps this is divine,

Perhaps it is all you.

I can see where I am going and what I must do;
Life is everything but meaningless thanks to you.

Cloudless Skies

Oh, if I could build you a greenhouse

A large and well protected area for you to flourish

Oh, if I could govern the sky above it

Make it unable to bear a cloud

Oh, if I could remould every piece of dirt on this planet

I would make it have the most perfect nutrient ratios

I would fill it with little bugs to maintain the ratio as well

Oh if I could

I would rebuild the whole world

I would make this place perfect for you

Precious Sunflower,

Even still the clouds cannot prevent you from blossoming

The Sun with Sunglasses

After a sun has lived and died,

After it has shined its last shines;

Does it wear sunglasses?

When its light is barely a whisper,

When the proof of its very existence begins to dwindle,

Does it wear sunglasses?

Does it hide away ashamed of what it could've been?

Does it regret abandoning the planets it sustained?

Does it wear sunglasses to protect itself

From its neighbours that shine even brighter than it ever did?

Do suns feel shame,

After they've burned dry,

And they've left their natural satellites in a cold, lifeless darkness?

Does my sun even know,

When it stopped shining and my inhabitants died,

My world became beautifully, peacefully silent?

When it shined itself out of existence,

When my sun brightly burned into a dark void,

It took with it the loud life on my planet.

Sunglasses Sun,

Don't ever remove your shades

Don't ever perceive the peace I have

For if you do,

If you perceive my very existence,

Your dull photons, will carry with them enough energy to reawaken this planet of mine.

I wish to remain dead to you.

I enjoy the silence.

Existing is peaceful without your noisy burning,

Without the loud voices of life.

Printed in Dunstable, United Kingdom